ANCHOR BOOKS

A LASTING IMAGE

Edited by

Heather Killingray

First published in Great Britain in 1999 by
ANCHOR BOOKS
Remus House,
Coltsfoot Drive,
Woodston,
Peterborough, PE2 9JX
Telephone (01733) 898101

All Rights Reserved

Copyright Contributors 1999

HB ISBN 1 85930 639 X
SB ISBN 1 85930 634 9

Foreword

Anchor Books is a small press, established in 1992, with the aim of promoting readable poetry to as wide an audience as possible.

We hope to establish an outlet for writers of poetry who may have struggled to see their work in print.

The poems presented here have been selected from many entries. Editing proved to be a difficult task and as the Editor, the final selection was mine.

I trust this selection will delight and please the authors and all those who enjoy reading poetry.

Heather Killingray
Editor

CONTENTS

Title	Author	Page
Rebirth	Shirley Sammout	1
Nature	Lauren Sammout	2
To Each Their Own	Eleanor Haydon Sanderson	3
A Christmas 'Pome'	Sylvia Westley	4
Everyone's A Poet	R Shurey	5
Concerns Every Person	Ghazanfer Eqbal	6
Writing Poems	Dee Dickens	7
Best Of British	A Kendall	8
Woodland Gallery	Lisa Cowap	9
A World For The Future	Naomi Kay	10
A World For The Future	Rebecca Foreman	11
Have An Ambition	Jenefer Livings	12
Think About It	Rebecca E Bugler	14
Hope	Melissa A George	15
For That Is In The Future	Kieran Balloo	16
What's Changed?	Amy Wright	17
War Games	Karen Munnings	18
Pollution	Kirsty Colyer	19
An Artificial Future	Helen Bourke	20
The Last Tree	Kimberley Edwards	21
Dream Island	Philippa Shallcross	22
A World For The Future!	Michael Ibrahim	23
Boys Are Nothing But Pains	Margaret-Louise Murphy	24
Boys	Tania Gepheart	25
Boys!	Jenny Powner	26
Boys	Catherine Brady	27
Me On Boys	Sarah Handley	28
My Favourite Thing Is . . . Football	Lynsey Evans	29
Sounds I Like	Sophie Warhurst	30
A World For The Future!	Dionne Lawrence	31
Boys	Chantelle O'Hara	32
Boring Boys	Melissa Noble	33
Boys	Laura Sharman	34
Boys Versus Girls	Kerry Winston	35
Some Girls, Some Boys	Roxanne Todd	36

Boys	Emily Forman	37
The Wonder Of Children	Jo Woolnough	38
Kailum 22 Months	Elizabeth Bell	39
Take Care	Mike Bradley	40
Mum	B Eyre	41
Babies' Ways And Beyond	Alma Montgomery Frank	42
Sweet Innocence	Margaret Jackson	43
The Flowers Of Dunblane	Haidee Williams	44
Little Blue Eyes	Angel Blue	45
Childhood Days	W Flitcroft	46
Shelly	T Baxter	47
Anne-Marie	H Young	48
What We Owe Children	Richard Stoker	49
Childhood Days	Vanessa Bell	50
Sally	John Clark	51
The Miracle	Val Spall	52
Don't Take Away Childhood	Kathryn Barkway	53
Daughter	Richard Reeve	54
The Perfect Gift	Pauline Hodson	55
Baby Days And Ways	Ruth Wright	56
To Ruth On Her Twelfth Birthday	Beryl Moorehead	57
The Passing Years	Jeanne Ison	58
The Magic Of Children	Audrey Allen	59
The Essence Of Spring	M Hanmer	60
The Lollipop Lady	K A Bayley	61
My Birthday Tribute	Roysden Tilley	62
A Poet's Ego	Alien 3	63
Crying On A Carousel Alone	Judy Studd	64
Forever Day	Dennis Studd	65
A Lovely Day	Jessie F Harper	66
High Cost Of Living	Lachlan Taylor	67
The Summer Of 'Sixty-Six	Sheila Burnett	68
I Love You . . . But	Gig	69
Village School (Chorley - 1983)	Irene G Corbett	70
Reflections	M J Scutter	71
The Environmentalist!	Alan Green	72
Death Within War	Amanda Rose	73

Homeless And Hungry	Rod Trott	74
God Is Divine	Kenneth Mood	75
Yellow Ochre	Sarah Margaret Munro	76
The Charity Shop	W Fred Tabaczynski	78
Is Your Confidence Misplaced?	Warren Brown	79
Shipwreck	Adrian Newport	80
Retirement	Keena	81
A Daughter's Love For Her Father	Farhana Hussain Begum	82
Facets Of A Horse	Hilary Jill Robson	83
The Photograph	Sandra Brisck	84
He Was On That Boat, The Hood	Tom Ritchie	85
Loneliness	Ben Morgan	86
People Being In Debt	Coleen Bradshaw	87
Jo - Simon	Evelyn Farr	88
Futility	Stan Short	89
The Day I Was So Scared	Antonio Martorelli	90
Protester	Bob Lewis	91
Spring Scene	Joan Taylor	92
Little Angels	Terry Daley	93
Pongamegunk	Janet Randall	94

REBIRTH

Build a bridge, not a burrow, look around.
Don't retreat into your tower, feet on the ground!
Cast the blinkers to one side, see the door it's open wide
No need to stay inside, sights abound!
'Sunday In The Park', see what I mean?
Stand back and be inspired by the scene.
The point's for all to find, saturate your mind
The harvest for Mankind is there to glean.
Skittering in the mire is not for you.
There's so much in this life to see and do,
Take time to meditate, then step outside the gate
No time to simply wait, go, see it through.
The world's a panorama, sight and sound,
Even on your doorstep can be found
Such a different view, it mesmerises you.
Leave behind the hare, to run with hound.
And when you've had your fill, no need to foot the bill,
Winding valley, highest hill, soaring bird, tallest tree,
The world and all you see, entwined with destiny,
A gift for ear and eye from earth to highest sky,
As far as you can see, until eternity,
Come in, it's waiting, wild and free
And, there's no need to pay an entrance fee.
Take a page out of My book, come in and take a look
Amen, so let it be . . . come with Me!

Shirley Sammout

NATURE

Sometimes I see the trees blow
And the leaves fall down . . .
And the clouds rain when they're sad,
That's when they dangle round.
When they cry, God makes them smile
And the world stays happy for a while.

Lauren Sammout (6)

TO EACH THEIR OWN

God bless and good luck to all who rave and rant
But not for modest me a huge boob implant
An inflated balloon chest I'd never ever want
I'd assuredly feel much like a cumbersome elephant
So thank you, no, to a silicone gel-based overblown enhancement
I'll stay content that mine are more affirmatively natural
And even sculpturesquely graceful and elegant.

Eleanor Haydon Sanderson

A Christmas 'Pome'

You need a child for Christmas, not more than six or seven,
Who still believes God sent a baby, Jesus, down from heaven.
Who rushes out from school to tell the great and glorious news
That he's a shepherd in the play, and can he have some shoes
Like shepherds wore in olden days, and then, when home you get,
The last thing that *he* wants to do is surf the Internet!
He's busy with some cushions and an ancient travelling rug,
Creating 'neath the table, a stable, warm and snug.
And all through tea he's on and on, when will his dad be home?
He wants to say his words to us, a poem, pronounced a 'pome'.
We're nagged up to the loft to get the decorations down,
Then he demands paper and glue to make some of his own.
Before he goes to bed at last, sophisticated though we be,
He has us in his stable, and there on bended knee,
We have to sing a carol, he knows the words quite well,
We're silent, as his childish voice the great glad tidings tell,
And glitzy office parties, the turkey, food and wine,
The need for costly presents, they all fade from the mind,
For all you need for Christmas is a child of six or seven,
Who makes you feel, just once a year, there is a God in Heaven.

Sylvia Westley

EVERYONE'S A POET

I do a bit of writing, to a certain extent, I have a free will,
If we go to war, although it will be against my will, I will,
Be forced to kill, I try not to offend with my writing, the material,
For thinkers is enormous, the world goes on to its fate, we are,
Bombarded with visions of wars, destruction, for some it is too late,
Why is there so much hate? Our lives are a vacuum and empty,
There is an aching void which only God can fill, He gives us joy and,
A hope of a better life to come, what is the point of going from,
Conception, to birth then old age and death to the grave?
Surely there must be more than that marble stone with our names,
In crisp gold letters carved out by the craftsman's hand, a plot in,
The ground, something more than that last journey through the,
Curtain to the fire, our ashes scattered to wherever we wished,
Them to be, placed in an urn on the mantelpiece or washed,
By the waves in the sea, God sent His only begotten Son to come,
To the earth, His church He bled and died to save, that is my hope,
In this howling wilderness, there must be more, to my way of,
Thinking, this world had nothing to offer me, I was empty and,
Black, weary and sad, life was a burden that I couldn't bear,
But then I met Jesus, He gives us peace and joy, we still,
Have problems, illness and pain, but we take them to God,
One day He has promised we will be with Him in Heaven,
We seem to be odd in this selfish callous world, Jesus was,
Hated and nailed to the tree, He tore strips off the religious,
Pharisee, it is not religion that will save us, but God's Son,
Who he gave us, the church has endured persecution,
Many have perished for their faith, but the church marches on,
Until all the world is gone, nothing goes on forever.

R Shurey

CONCERNS EVERY PERSON

Every corner perhaps
there is a cry for free enterprise
it did exist in the past
it is not perfect
it has its pitfalls
so every person must not forget it
in every moment every day's
kaleidoscopic life's livings

So no person ever should dream
to slowly destroy the welfare state
and National Health Service of the nation

I admire the brain that conceived it
planned it executed it
as it is gradually eroded and destroyed
A financially better off person may lose money
and a poor person could become rich . . . well off
So these nets are essential for every person
British have done it in the past
So the present and the future not only
should be endeavoured
but preserved for each generation to come
pointing and educating the beauty
the economy of it to every person

Ghazanfer Eqbal

WRITING POEMS

I like to think in the day,
When my mind can wander away,
Writing poems can be real fun,
Thinking of things that you've done.

It's amazing all the things you think,
When you're relaxed with a drink,
Writing your poems, just for fun,
Hoping no disturbances come along.

Putting pen to paper, is easy to do,
You just need to have a little clue,
What to write, might come to you,
If you know about something new.

Titles are easy, they just come to mind,
It's just the verses you have to find,
Writing them, rhyming them, line to line,
Poem writing relaxes your mind.

Letters come through the door,
I wonder whom they are for,
A letter for me, let's have a look,
My poem's been accepted for a book.

All excited, I get a buzz,
This is what poem writing does,
Entering poems for a book,
So everyone can read and look.

Dee Dickens

BEST OF BRITISH

Within our green and pleasant land,
Our British Bulldog lurks,
It plods along against all odds,
And nothing does it shirk.

Up and down our country,
Wherever we may roam,
We love our British ways and means,
And always land back home.

Roaming round the Dales,
Walking up the hills,
Calling back for fish and chips,
And paying all our bills.

Strolling through our country lanes,
Upon a summer's day,
Seeing all the trees and flowers,
As we pass on our way.

So we may press on apace,
Up to London town,
To see so much that's British,
That comes into its own.

Our stately buildings proudly stand,
A heritage so great,
A city steeped in history,
A story it does make.

The British flag flies over all,
So proudly in the breeze,
And people come from near and far,
To witness all of these.

A Kendall

WOODLAND GALLERY

Soft sunshine penetrating through rough, rugged trees,
Twisting, entwining slender branches,
Sturdy, mighty tree trunks,
Starting to decay,
Filling the moss-covered base of the captivating woodland,
Minibeasts scavenge for food in immense ferns,
Thick gooey mud grabbing anything that steps out
delicately onto it,
Brown stale leaves plunging tenderly to the violent,
uneven ground,
Fine bark flaking then tumbling off a lifeless tree,
Unspoilt by man,
The forest lives on.

Lisa Cowap (11)

A World For The Future

A world for the future,
What does it mean?
Our world in turmoil, bursting at the seams,
An hour's drive to see a tree,
Or alternatively,
Trees and green grass
A plant or a flower.
What must we say to the people in power
To make them realise our fear?
The time is now, the moment's here!

Naomi Kay (12)

A WORLD FOR THE FUTURE

Is where there is peace,
and no more war,

Where people are kind
to one another,

Animals are free from people
hurting them,

And the environment
is free from pollution,

That's what I would like
for my future.

Rebecca Foreman (11)

HAVE AN AMBITION

What will happen?
No one knows
Speculate and hope
Have an ambition

Be who you want
Rich, famous, me,
Imagine your wish
Have an ambition

Meet the one
Far or near
Is he? Maybe?
Have an ambition

Get the job,
Set the goal,
Show yourself, you can
Have an ambition

Daydreaming? No!
Just planning vision
A notion? Yes!
Have an ambition

A reverie, a fantasy
Fate destined, for you
Hope and expectation
Have an ambition

Have an illusion
Have a fantasy
Reverie and imagine
Have an ambition

Have an ambition
Make it be true
Your dream, your vision,
Can be you!

Jenefer Livings (15)

THINK ABOUT IT

The wildlife won't last forever,
The nature and the people,
The nature dying off in pairs,
The people getting old and grey,
The fruit of love and ambition,
The breathing of the bugs of life,
And the trees blossoming in the breeze,
Mankind will all be gone in years to come,
The sea will have drowned,
The sky will have flown,
The clouds will have evaporated,
The sun will have melted,
The moon disappeared,
Grass just dead,
So think about it,
No trees for shade,
No grass where we played,
No people to talk to,
No stars to look up to,
No sun to warm to,
So just think how it would be,
If I were you and you were me.

Rebecca E Bugler (11)

Hope

Never lose hope,
No matter what life throws at you,
No matter who deceives you,
Never lose hope!

If you're hurting and crying,
If you're lonely and sad,
However life should test you,
Never lose faith!

If the world seems against you,
Remember my words,
If your friends seem to hate you,
Remember my words.

Your hopes and your dreams
Will all soon come true,
You will then remember
What I said to you.

Never lose hope!

Melissa A George (16)

For That Is In The Future

I go to sleep each night,
and wonder what tomorrow will be like,
for that is in the future.

But what about in one month's time?
A year, a decade, a century's time?
For that is in the future.

So will we live on Earth at all?
On Mars, a spaceship, the moon?
For that is in the future.

Then I open my eyes,
And now today is tomorrow.
But what will tomorrow be like?
For that is in the future.

Kieran Balloo (15)

What's Changed?

The churchyard stands empty and grey
like the homeless and old
empty of love, warmth
full only of memories

As memories to others
they are no longer known
history
there's no going back
everything's new

New family, friends
out with the old and in with the new
for we are in the past
we are ancient history
only memories

Our places filled
with those younger, brighter
for we were once there
but our welcome outstayed
out with the old and in with the new.

Amy Wright (16)

War Games

Innocent blood spilled onto the hands of evil.
The scent of life lost into the welcoming poppies, that bloom there,
not knowing.
Showers of screams
fading into the silence of memory.
Loneliness. Suffering. Moaning of wolves in front howling as
if someone could hear them.
Soft voices shattering the ground below.
Cries of mothers fussing.
Fussing for their families, looking for their warm children
produced from their lost one deep inside.
Bullets flashing like birds of prey, piercing the soft skin
of beauty, deep in the souls of many.
Painful moments of loss, united only in imaginary visions from
the soul.
Shouting men of those uniforms. Fields of dreams shattered
their lives, faded silence.
Wailing of evil, deepened by the loud danger sounds.
Danger.
Run to cover.
Bombs dropped on innocent homes.
Given no choice but to play in the sick challenge between
life or death.

Every face hides a past.
Every past hides the future.
Every future worries the world.

Karen Munnings (16)

POLLUTION

Pollution is what's in the air
On your clothes, your face, your hair
It isn't very nice you know
To have pollution wherever you go

But lots of people do not care
They don't even know it's there
Lots of it is factories
Damaging the air we breathe

A clear future we can see
It won't be a pleasant place to be
But if we all use bikes instead of a car or a bus
The world would be cleaner for all of us

Kirsty Colyer (10)

An Artificial Future

What will the 'wonderful' future hold?
Faster cars, of course,
and plenty more sold.
But at what price?
There'll be more road traffic accidents,
and gridlock galore.
More teenage drivers, but more teenage drinkers.

What will the 'wonderful' future hold?
Brand new discoveries.
New animals untold.
But at what price?
They'll find a new species,
but endanger four more.
More conservation plans, but more forests destroyed.

What will the 'wonderful' future hold?
A new supermodel craze.
Old sizes, left out in the cold.
But at what price?
There'll be more unattainable dreams,
the new size is four.
More supermodels, but more eating disorders.

What will the 'wonderful' future hold?
Easier operations.
As the doctors' plans unfold.
But at what price?
There'll be a new silicone era,
Lose your true identity for sure.
More beautiful people, but more artificial love.

Helen Bourke

THE LAST TREE

Surrounded by an electric fence,
in a military base.
Stands The Last Tree.

Crowds gather.
The clink of money sounds,
and a machine spits out tickets
All for The Last Tree.

The sun has set,
the crowds are gone.
The Last Tree is alone.

A silent tear trickles down its trunk
for all its long dead ancestors and dead world.
Then all life is gone
The Last Tree is no more.

Kimberley Edwards

Dream Island

An ocean of blue,
sand falls around you like raindrops.
Treasures gleam like the shining sun,
even the oldest clouds look new.

No one is sad,
There are no wars or fights,
No greed or selfishness,
for this you are glad.

The mystical sky,
enchanting everyone,
Holding in place the much-loved sun.
You love to sit and look up high.

Open your eyes, it's just a dream,
The real world is polluted.
We are greedy, money is life.
People are mean.

Philippa Shallcross (13)

A WORLD FOR THE FUTURE!

Now the sunrise,
2000 just round the corner,
People say the end is near,
People say there'll be big bugs of fear,
Who knows?

2000 a year of joy,
Or despair,
Maybe Armageddon was a prophecy,
Not just a Hollywood movie.

I've always wanted a dog,
Maybe 2000 will give me one,
Or maybe they'll die out,
And be replaced with giant Tamagotchis.

Who knows?

Michael Ibrahim

BOYS ARE NOTHING BUT PAINS

Boys are pains,
Boys are vain,
Boys are boring; they're all the same.

Boys are dumb,
Boys are stupid,
Boys aren't any fun,
They hate the sun.

Boys are aggravating,
Boys are trouble,
There is no word for these monstrous things,
All I can say is boys are nothing but pains.

Margaret-Louise Murphy (14)

BOYS

Boys are lazy, scruffy too,
Football crazy, what's new!
Cheats in tests, they never confess,
That is what I think of boys.

Tania Gepheart (8)

Boys!
(Who'd have 'em?)

Do they come from Mars?
Do they come from Uranus?
Cos they're *not* from Earth!

They *can't* be from Earth!
They are not clever enough!
They are aliens!

Surely you can see!
They're *so* different from us.
Real boys don't exist!

Jenny Powner (11)

Boys

My baby boy all dressed in blue
Completely changed before he was two
He screams and shouts and breaks his toys
Then picks on all the girls and boys

At four years old to school he goes
To sit in a room with no one he knows
He sits all day as quiet as a mouse
Then once he's home he wrecks my house

At six years old they say he's bright
I just wish he'd sleep at night
His life is full of fun and games
With lots of friends with different names

At ten years old he's footie mad
Watching TV all day with his dad
I've shown him the Hoover and the duster too
And each time I do this he just runs to the loo

Now he's a teenager my hair's turning grey
With the amount of money he asks for each day
I think now my troubles have only just started
If he carries on like this I'll soon be departed

Catherine Brady (10)

ME ON BOYS

Me on boys neither good nor bad,
but don't you think that they're really sad?
I don't know about you but I certainly do.

Boys can't cope with handling soap,
nor handle girls alone,
because we're cool, the coolest in school
and we're the ones that rule.
Boys like footie, I wonder why?
They're always on about a flippin' guy.
Most of them I've never known,
like Shearer, Beckham and Michael Owen.
Are they good or are they bad?
I don't know cos I'm not a lad.

Me on boys neither good nor bad,
but don't you think that they're really sad?
I don't know about you but I certainly do.
So now I hope that you've changed your view.

Sarah Handley

MY FAVOURITE THING IS... FOOTBALL

Football! Football! Shouting out aloud,
I'm running down the pitch waving to the crowd.
I've scored a goal, a free kick in fact,
Now I have become the leader of the pack.
When I kicked the ball I hoped and prayed,
That the ball would hit the net someday.
When it finally did I let out a scream,
That this goal had answered my dream.

Lynsey Evans

SOUNDS I LIKE

I like the sound of
the clash of thunder
that roars
like a giant
I like the sound of
peace and quiet
nice quiet
whispering
waves at the seaside
the trees rustling in the wind
the sound of my brakes on my bike squealing
the sound of my friends
running to my door
and Lindsay's bike rattling to my gate.

Sophie Warhurst

A World For The Future!

The world, the world, is a beautiful place,
With lots and lots and lots of space.
Though some people are quite cruel,
And some people are really fools.
In this world are people who are rich,
And some that are poor,
And some that are in the middle.
We have a lot of pollution,
And lots of people jump to conclusions.
That's the thing about the world,
We all make a lot of mistakes.

Dionne Lawrence

Boys

Boys, boys, boys,
Don't play with toys.
Some play football,
Some play basketball.

Boys, boys, boys,
Don't play with toys.
Some play games,
With all different names.

Chantelle O'Hara (8)

BORING BOYS

B oys are boring.
O nly out to annoy.
Y our brother's the worst.
S ure to pinch your toy.

Boys – yuk!

Melissa Noble (10)

Boys

The trouble with my brother is,
He's naughty all the time,
He doesn't put away his toys,
And often pinches mine.

He's always in a mardy mood,
If he can't get his own way,
I try to be real nice to him,
But he just says 'Go away.'

The trouble is I love him,
He's the only brother I have,
I just wish he wasn't so naughty,
But good and kind not
        Bad.

Laura Sharman (10)

BOYS VERSUS GIRLS

Boys are too lazy to have jobs
They just sit around like slobs
They sit in front of you and pick their nose
Not to mention their toes
When they go to a party they don't dress up
They would rather be covered in muck

Girls are nice and polite
And they are always right
We can play football better than any old boy can
And we use a ball not a tin can
You may think we are nancies
But we are the ones that everyone fancies

But after all that I will say
I would like to be a boy just for one day.

Kerry Winston (11)

SOME GIRLS, SOME BOYS

Some girls can be nasty
Some girls can be sweet
Some girls wear make-up
And others dress for boys they meet

Some boys can be a pain
Some boys can be nice
Some boys talk about themselves
And others talk about Posh Spice

Some girls like to play tennis
Some girls play netball
Some girls shop at Tammy
And others prefer The Mall

Some boys like to play cricket
Some boys play football
Some boys like fixing things
And others like to do nothing at all.

Roxanne Todd

BOYS

Boys are rough and tough
Fighting all day long
They're only interest is football
And running about
They're silly and they're weird.
They really spook me out.

Emily Forman (10)

THE WONDER OF CHILDREN

As babies we watch you grow,
like the farmer watching the seed he sows.
We see you toddle and watch you fall,
knowing that you will soon walk tall.

Hearing the laughter and watching you cry,
brings a teardrop to our eyes.
You have such energy, so much get up and go.
So many questions and answers to know.

Children all over go through the stages,
from infancy to the teen ages.
Each is different, each unique,
like learning a new language, a new tongue to speak.

Just like the baby bird learning to fly,
we watch you learning and watch you try.
Every day is a new challenge, a new mystery,
and you attempt it with a smile all can see.

We all know they are precious, we all feel the joy,
holding a new baby, be it a girl or a boy.
Of knowing we helped bring a new life into this world,
amazed as this tiny life slowly unfurls.

All around the world we watch the babies become full grown,
knowing they are maturing and able to have children of their own.
The circle of life keeps turning, millions of babies born each day,
and the children of tomorrow will be parents themselves one day!

Jo Woolnough

KAILUM 22 MONTHS

Nana knows that Kailum loves her,
But doesn't stand a chance,
He only sees his Grandad
With eyes that flash and dance.

Grandad, water greenhouse,
Where the lettuce grow,
It's Kailum's greenhouse Grandad,
Thought I'd just let you know.

Grandad, see the birdies,
Yellow, green and blue,
Grandad call for Will-ee-am,
Faith and Colin too.

Grandad play at hide and seek,
Grandad play the band,
Grandad, march around the room,
With spoon and dish to bang.

Grandad, Grandad, uppy stairs,
Kailum jump on bed,
Nana says to Kailum 'No,
No jumpy on the bed.'

Grandad, Grandad, Grandad,
Will it ever end?
But Grandad's not just Grandad,
He's Kailum's bestest friend.

Elizabeth Bell

TAKE CARE

Children are not just born to annoy
So share their trials and tribulations
Parenthood should be a pleasure, a joy
Enjoin them in negotiations
Treat them with compassion and understanding, do not stem
Enjoy your offsprings and be content
What is trivia to us, can be disastrous to them
They are yours, you brought them, they were not sent
Raise those offsprings to some better life
Be strong and bold with the standards you set
Give them love, care, not strife
Above all, be fair, your wishes can be met
Understand too that things do change
As time progresses, extend your range.

Mike Bradley

Mum

Mum! Have you washed my PE kit?
I need it today for school.
Mum! Have I got a clean shirt?
A white one, that's the rule.

Mum Have you seen my trainers?
I left them on the floor.
Mum! Can me mate come in and wait?
He's standing at the door.

Mum! Have you seen my homework?
I left it on the hall stand.
Mum! I need some new shoes.
Please say that I can.

Mum! I'm staying for football practice,
And won't be home till six.
Mum! I've broken my radio,
I'll leave it for you to fix.

Mum! Can I have my dinner money?
The bus is at the gate.
Mum! Have you seen my bus pass?
Quick or I'm going to be late.

Mum! Thanks for everything.
He said as he went out the door.
As she stood and sighed, she reflected.
'That's just what mums are for!'

B Eyre

Babies' Ways And Beyond

Never a dull moment
When our babies are around
Into everything seen by their eyes
They are sure to crawl straight for mum's special vase
It is never too high they can't reach
Crash! Not there soon enough to stop the breakage
Babies laugh with joy
You just can't lay a finger on them
It's a case of laughing with them the young imps
But there are times in their youth
When shadows overpower them with destruction
Of body and soul these sadists are lurking in dark allies
Waiting to pounce upon them
Use their positive evil skills
Then kill the goodness that was in the youths' hearts
With a treacherous white pill or powder
It isn't long before things
Turn to wrongful deaths
We parents do our level best
To keep them on the straight and narrow
We often don't know what is going on
Until too late
Please don't blame us
Don't put it on our 'trying plate'
If only we had known in time
Prevention is better than cure
May this poem be a warning
To parents all
I now wish you everlasting luck and more

Alma Montgomery Frank

Sweet Innocence

The gift of love, a babe so small
perfect in every way.
Sweet innocence before our eyes
bringing much joy each day.

Magical moments always share
children's laughter delight.
Imaginations travel far
fantasy world so bright.

First words to speak and steps to take
knowing someone is there.
To hold their hand and keep them safe
much tender love and care.

Little ways never to forget
helping, trying to please.
Gleam twinkling stars beneath the skies
then mischief make to tease.

Great their trust, offering such love
hugs, cuddles to impart.
Soon bouncing back through tears and pain
special within our heart.

Sunny smiles captivate us all
such excitement anew.
These precious blessings in our arms
fulfilment glows so true.

Margaret Jackson

THE FLOWERS OF DUNBLANE

Like flowers in an early frost
The children of *Dunblane* were lost.
They'd gone to school to sing and play
But this was no ordinary day.
Evil walked in through the door
And left them lying on the floor.
The day the flowers of *Dunblane* died
The world hung its head - and cried.

Haidee Williams

LITTLE BLUE EYES

I miss you little blue eyes. My heart still calls your name.
I see you in my dreams, but we know it's not the same.
I cannot hold you to my breast, nor soothe your troubled sleep.
The pain burns on, as fast, as ever deep.
Sitting in your room, I can smell you in the air.
The hair spray, and the gel, and the perfume that we shared.
I knew that you would go one day, as all children have to leave,
but not go so finally and leave me here to grieve.
You said that you were popping out, that you'd be back by four.
At three twenty-seven pm that knock came at the door.
I knew before I answered, that my world had fell apart.
A mother doesn't need police to feel a shattered heart.
I miss you little blue eyes. But I know just what to do,
if you can't come to Mummy, then Mummy will come to you.

Angel Blue

CHILDHOOD DAYS

I remember well my childhood days
When I sat on Mother's knee
She would croon to me a lullaby
Or say a nursery rhyme to me.
She taught me how to kneel and pray
To my God above
A God who loves all children
The God that we all love.
And if I fell who was always there
To kiss away my tears
Told me wonderful bedtime stories
To drive away my fears.
A mother who was always there
To teach me right from wrong
Who told me 'It is wrong to steal,
Put things back where they belong.'
I really miss my mother now
She's gone to Heaven above,
I'd like to grow up just like her
An angel filled with love.

W Flitcroft

SHELLY

Fists, eyes and nose screwed up tight
Tiny foot stamping with all its might.
Who is this ferocious three year old
That doesn't want to do what she's told?

It's 'Shelly', the silver-haired angel
My tender nurse when I was disabled,
Lifting my legs with gentle care
Placing them on her own little chair,
Passing my pen, a blanket or book
Ensuring my tablets and potions, I took.

Bright as a button, nobody's fool,
A staunch believer in self-rule,
With such compassion and determination
I guess she'll grow up to be quite a sensation.

T Baxter

ANNE-MARIE

You are a beautiful child,
and the way you hold onto me
makes me feel as if you are mine,
as if you are the joyful product
of my love with some unseen other.

Your laughter delights me
and I struggle to hide my adoration.
I would circle your little form forever
in the warmth of my arms
did I not feel guilty
claiming you from another.

I wish I were your father
and you my never-ageing daughter.
The gentle caress of the smoothness of your hand
tiny in mine, carelessly touching
would occupy my life forever.
Your smile would fulfil my days
and I would happily listen
to a tiny voice reassuring me in the darkness.

H Young

WHAT WE OWE CHILDREN

Children rest always in our thoughts
We owe them all immeasurable things
They owe us life itself
We owe them peace and happiness
The pitfalls cruel dangerous ways *we* know
Most of these they've yet to discover
To help them on their way as if unaided
Should be our one-time goal
We owe them all so much
Is love enough to give and life?
Life like plants needs nurturing

Richard Stoker

CHILDHOOD DAYS

Childhood is beautiful
A time of joy and innocence
Of happiness and wonder
A special time in every sense

A time of rough and tumble
Riding bikes and climbing trees
Being boisterous, getting dirty
Flying kites and grazing knees

Building sandcastles on holiday
Playing in the autumn leaves
Joyful laughter fills the air
Faces shining, bright and happy

Playing football in the park
Witches and ghosts at Hallowe'en
Fairy tales, the bogeyman
Handsome princes, eating ice-cream

Building snowmen, going sledging
Shouts and squeals, playing snowballs
Tingling toes and tingling fingers
Faces aglow, watching snow fall

Writing letters to Santa Claus
Telling him the presents that you want
Leave him a mince pie and some sherry
And a carrot for Rudolph

Playing conkers in the school yard
The Tooth Fairy, Man in the Moon
Our childhood is a magical time
That disappears all too soon

Vanessa Bell

SALLY

In her scarlet jumper
and her denim jeans.
That's my daughter Sally
battling through her teens.

Sometimes quite a woman
sometimes just a girl
with half-a-dozen boyfriends,
emotions in a whirl.

Seldom stops indoors now
hardly touches down.
Home from school, a hasty snack
then she's off to town.

Dancing at the disco
stopping out quite late.
How we worry till we
hear her at the gate.

Where's that little girl gone
who once sat on my knee?
Now she's like a stranger,
seldom speaks with me.

Soon she'll be a woman
teenage fads outgrown.
She'll settle down and marry -
have babies of her own.

Maybe she will understand
as her children grow.
Why we parents worry
and how we love her so.

John Clark

THE MIRACLE

A mouth wat'ring meal devoured, but quick as a wink
the whole lot was disgorged into the sink!
Could it be salmonella or gastro perhaps?
Or that jaundice last year - in a relapse?

The next morning was a repeat of the same routine
with aching stomach and face turning green.
Then a vague suspicion replaced my anxious care
could there perhaps be a baby in there?

A flood of emotion, then rush for the test.
It was really true! My mind now at rest.
Could a sweet little child really be inside
or some gruesome monster, trying to hide?

Zips that won't fasten, ever increasing weight gain!
Blue stretch marks wiggle like worms in the rain!
Craving for ice-cream in the middle of the night.
Moods that switch on and off like the light.

Use lanolin dear, take your calcium too.
Don't worry! There'll soon be a nice slim you!
What's this! I'm all wet! My back is stabbed with a knife.
Twenty minutes! Ten minutes! Hello strife!

Just one final push, your cries tell me you are here.
I scan your body as I hold you near.
No monster this! But a beautiful son.
A miracle, when the labour is done.

Your tiny body, an inspiration indeed
fulfilling every conceivable need.
A book of life opens, with pages unfurled
and a precious son enters the world!

Val Spall

Don't Take Away Childhood

I'm small I know,
All I do isn't liked by you,
I can't see I don't understand,
Yet you yell at me so.

I want to relate,
To be good and not irritate,
You don't let me,
You just say no.

Toys are such fun,
Even learning to run,
I know I want,
I know I'm a pain.

But won't you hear,
I'm fed up with this,
I want to be free,
To live as a child.

Not one of you,
I don't know enough,
I only know to be me,
Oh! Can't you see?

Please don't yell so,
Give me some space,
Let me show you,
I'll grow.

Then I'll be like you,
Not that child no more,
You'll miss me then,
I want to be me,
Can't you see?

Kathryn Barkway

DAUGHTER

We fed you, girl, from what we had
and did not forget the *Virol*.
We bought you shilling Golden Books
and pushed you in a too big pram
or carried you on shoulder's high
and did not forget the *Virol*.
We made a playground in the yard
and watched you play with baited breath,
risking your young adventures
and feared for you when at school.
But the greatest thing we gave was love
and did not forget the *Virol*.

Richard Reeve

THE PERFECT GIFT

The seeds of love are sown in the womb
a precious new life to grow very soon.
Nature provides all the care till it's born
inside Mum's tummy all cosy and warm.
How can this baby fit into this space
and develop as part of the human race.

A child is a gift, the most precious of all
nothing prepares for this feeling of awe.
Their sweet little smile can make your heart flip
sharing your home in their own little crib.
To watch them progress to a small little you
are moments to treasure and wonderfully new.

They bring out the love that God did intend
and this special love will never end.
Through all their childhood and adulthood too
they will always be a part of you.

Their eyes they sparkle on special days
Christmas, birthdays or going away.
Their excitement with a first picture they draw
and for a reaction your face they explore.
Born little comics they bring such joy
little people - girl or boy.

Pauline Hodson

BABY DAYS AND WAYS

All children are so special
a gift from God above.
So hug each child with pleasure
and shower them with love.

Shining eyes watch bubbles
glistening in the air.
Bobbing balloons and birthday cake
for everyone to share.

Fairy tales and nursery rhymes
rainbow in the sky.
Spinning tops and candyfloss
a gentle lullaby.

These magic days are fleeting
one day they'll be far gone.
Remember happy moments
and cherish every one.

Ruth Wright

TO RUTH ON HER TWELFTH BIRTHDAY

A peach bloom baby with petal soft skin
and down for hair and a sweet mouth and chin.
So much joy to watch you grow, to toddle and run.
How we loved you so.
Inquisitive fingers and bright little eyes
an adventurous spirit and full of surprise.

A grave little schoolgirl, so neat and trim
hiding a tear and a fear within.
Mother must leave you and teacher begin
to enlarge your view of the world you're in.

A world which contained an unpleasant surprise
an ordeal which forced us to lift our eyes
and seek for strength in an unseen Power.
To meet the needs of our darkest hour
but God was with us and you came through.
An eleventh summer we shared with you.

And now you're twelve and a joy to behold,
like a rose to the sun you begin to enfold.
I hope you will shed a fragrance, a sheen.
An aura, a sense of a radiance unseen,
I long for a *Spirit-filled* woman to grow
and merge from that baby we both loved so.

Beryl Moorehead

The Passing Years

I look in the nursery and what do I see?
A little pink baby gurgling at me.
Her fluffy white rabbit and other soft things
Oh, what a joy a small baby brings.

But time goes fast, already she's walking.
It won't be long now and she will be talking.
She gives me a cuddle with little plump arms
How I enjoy her babyish charms.

I look round the room and what do I see?
Dolls and teddy bears looking at me.
Where the years go to, I really don't know
But look at my children, see how they grow.

As the years pass what do I find?
Toys of a very different kind.
Records and tapes of their favourite stars,
Powder and lipstick in numerous jars.

School books and papers litter the floor.
Oh gosh! I can't pick them up any more.
Exams are all finished, career times begin
Whatever they tackle I pray they will win.

I look at my daughter and what do I see?
A lovely young woman smiling at me.
She looks so serene as she waits patiently
The birth of her baby, how radiant is she.

When a small baby smiles everything is just fine,
Just like a ray of warm summer sunshine.
I remember my babies and when they first smiled.
Oh, how I look forward to my little grandchild.

Jeanne Ison

THE MAGIC OF CHILDREN

Take a class of children
no matter what age.
Tell them of a magic wood
see adventure conjured up.
Their imagination is inspiring -
from the classroom floor
springs a cave, a bridge, a tree.
Guarded by a giant, witch,
even a dinosaur or two; where can they hide?
The gentle competition - was I the best?
Generous applause from everyone
when someone does quite well.
It seems hard to believe that only last week
they were too shy to come through the door
and now, a hook to get them off the floor.
Then comes the real magic,
that tiny hand, pushed into yours,
as they offer you their love.
The smile that says it all.
Yes! How we love to fantasise,
to be a flying bat, to change into a rat.
To work with one another.
Childhood is very special,
for the young and for the old.
Especially for the young at heart.

Audrey Allen

The Essence Of Spring

The primrose is a crinoline lady.
Crocuses are like a parasol opening wide.
Fragrant violets love it nice and shady.
Primulas have peaches and cream centres inside.
Majestic polyanthus are a heart's delight.
Polka-dot pansies bloom in yellow mauve and reds.
Violas look so fragile in pearl white.
Anemones have frilly heads
But the narcissus is like the queen of May.
Attended by her ladies fair and waited upon
give's a lovely display.
Trumpets the daffodil into golden song
reaching upward to the sun.
All dressed up for a ball again.
Whispering breezes rustle petals in fun
Entrance they appear by falling rain.
As diamond pendants cling and hold
reflections make jewelled lights in ruby amber rare.
Bringing joy untold
But none can compare.
In the magic of the flowers I tend.
Planted in my garden I love so.
Where I mix match and blend
from the seeds I sow.
Enriching my garden more
amidst the cornflowers blue that waivers.
Dotted in and out the bluebells tall.
Where mysterious silver traces are left on leaves
but in pride of place stands the cherry tree where
from within, comes the blackbird song rejoicing in
the very essence of spring.

M Hanmer

THE LOLLIPOP LADY

My friend the lollipop lady
how you have to stop and think.
The kids are enough to drive you to drink.
We can see you coming with your bright fluorescent coat.
But you always seem to be smiling and acting the goat.
You're standing in the road with your big lollipop stick.
But no-one ever asks you for a lick.
So never mind! Don't get in a bind.
Because you're one of a kind . . .

K A Bayley

My Birthday Tribute

I want to send a birthday card to Heaven.
A message to a dear old friend of mine
the skies above are damp - and the moisture on the stamp
just might affect the writing on each line.

I want to say *a happy birthday - Brother*
and are they looking after you up there?
It's hard for me to post a letter to a ghost
not knowing if a card's allowed up there!

I'd like to say *I miss you* - but you know that anyway
I'll tell you things are fine down here, and I might even say.
It doesn't seem too long ago - but time has passed away
and tomorrow is your very special day.

But if my message can't get through by way of normal post
I'll still convey my words to you through time's Eternal host.
I know he'll wish you all that my heart wishes you the most.
To this precious day in time -my very special toast.

Time goes by and ages fly and great loves come and go
but we still never really lose the ones we've come to know.
So God will pluck my birthday card and pass it on to you
for that's the sort of thing that God would do.
And he will give my blessing straight to you.

Roysden Tilley

A Poet's Ego

Have you heard about poet of the year?
Stand well back and I'll make it clear.
The title is mine as I want some ego
The country will know from top to toe.

Read my poem first, it is the best.
I can do better than all the rest.
Poet's only like to have a laugh.
Having this title will show that I'm not daft.

Right everyone! Let's have some fun.
Publish my poem and it will do the trick.
Soon they will read poems out in the editor's journal *The Sun* . . .
Then that will make everyone's brain tick.

Choice from the editor is final
Whatever the cost please do not get suicidal.
Competitions are hard to compete in
but most of all everyone has *ego* to *win*.

Alien 3

CRYING ON A CAROUSEL ALONE

Searching for existence in the puzzle that is me.
I try to find reality; a reason just to be.
Do I wear a smile today; do I wear a frown?
Shall I scream and shout today or shall I be a clown?

Will I have some purpose to take me through the day,
in this meaningless existence, will I find my way?
I want to show my anger; I want to show my pain
yet when I try to be myself, I'm knocked down once again.

The maze of life's confusion leaves me right out on a limb
the search for true identity has made my vision dim.
This crazy world we love to hate has left me standing still
there must be meaning somewhere this aching void to fill.

I need to search for answers but - where do I begin?
A creature of captivity securely bolted in.
The people who are close to me may think that all is well
is there a key to turn this lock - release me from my cell?

So - it's either on a soapbox or turn the other cheek
would that make me strong as steel; would it make me weak?
Truth and confrontation might get me through the fight
but ships on alien courses float aimlessly through night.

There is one conflict left to choose; silence or speech
both contained within my grasp yet simply out of reach.
Silence shall be golden when truth alone is told
I will discard my mask today - risk it and be bold.

Judy Studd

FOREVER DAY

On the mountains of your covenant, the icy winds sweep down, carrying with them the winter snows of confusion.

With clarity of vision, I stand alone, mocked by uncertainty. Doubt, like some great vulture, hands suspended in the caverns of my mind, awaiting the death of reason; but the time for joy is not yet passed. Freedom's fighter beckons, and my heart soars on wings of worship, carrying me to where the eagle dares to fly; blinded by the sun. Yet my wings are weak and immature, and my feathers are still downy.

How can I reach my Lord, 'midst the granite of my heart?

The rocks around tower o'er me, yet I am not afraid. The silver rocks glint in the passion of my emotions; yet feelings disturb. These are not the way. Your heart cries to me, its sound bounces against the fragile canyons, and falls weeping. And I stand alone; again alone, reaching out, crying for the peace of heart that denies reason. Again my wings reach out; I stand again at the cliff's very edge, seeking the way aloft.
But I see only down. Down, down, to where the rivers of the canyon of death tumble and spit below me. But I must try. I reach out, and the winds of reason batter me again. Yet suddenly a touch; a whisper, so distant, so soft, I barely sense its meaning; and gone, I leave the cliff. It's done. Far below the river's spray seems torture to my heart; yet far beyond, your gentle hand beckons softly; and I fly! Soaring aloft, leaving the icy winds below me, the granite of my heart hidden by your hand, I'm free! And your love draws me onward, ever upward, to where the sun shines eternally, forever day.

Dennis Studd

A Lovely Day

It was the merry, merry month named May.
Three minstrels and poet Will came this way
Walking, talking they music made.
Nearing Welford on Avon's 'cottage of content'
They opened door and inside went.
'Landlord' had for them a meal prepared.
Pigeon pie a tasty dish, with golden crust.
Plum pudding of ripe yellow - one's quite filling
With this a jug of home-brewed brown ale.
Replete happy, it's 'gone to their heads'
They quietly to settle in corner make tread.
Soon fell asleep it was closing time
The landlord's good wife said
'Let's shut that door and let 'em doze.
For it's merry, merry they be - it's gone to their toes!'

Jessie F Harper

HIGH COST OF LIVING

Those high prices here in Britain
is something we don't need.
It can only be our businessmen
who are so imbued by greed.

Take cigarettes, drink and petrol
cars and worst still - food.
We pay much more than anyone
throughout Europe's neighbourhood.

I have tried to find an answer here
as it is hard to understand.
The difference in our prices
compared to other lands.

We beat those other countries
as far as wealth and riches go.
Is this due to those high prices
I believe this to be so.

I recall America was lost to us
and high taxes were to blame.
It seems they have never learned a lesson
for still they do the same.

Lachlan Taylor

The Summer of 'Sixty-Six
(With Apologies to Edward Thomas and 'Adlestrop')

Yes. I remember 'sixty-six -
the summer, because one afternoon
in August our son was born;
it happened not a moment too soon.

The final push; I heard a cry;
in that second everything changed -
we now were three! A family!
A sixties' life-style rearranged.

And this small baby (not so small)
who looked at me with eyes, deep blue,
had brought about a seismic shift,
the like of which he little knew.

Outdoors was sunshine warm and bright
and men and women strolling free;
indoors, a green delivery room
and just we two, my son and me.

Sheila Burnett

I Love You . . . But

I love you . . . but
I'm not rich, or famous just ordinary.
I laugh, I cry,
One day I'll die
Please accept me for who I am.

I love you . . . but
I'm not clever, or dumb.
No desire to be under the thumb
I'm no angel or saint.
Never try to be, who I ain't
I try to be good, yet often I'm bad
Sometimes sorry, sometimes sad.

I love you . . . but
If I'm cut, I bleed
Don't go to church, yet I believe
Do not place me on a pedestal.
Think twice before you're nice
I can change, so if you still want me
I'll be faithful and true
And always love you . . . but

Gig

VILLAGE SCHOOL (CHORLEY - 1983)

In a quiet little village, a few miles out of town.
Is a lovely little school, although sadly, they're going to close it down.
They say its children are too few, but it seems such a pity
when you remember, all those children
whom go to school in the city.
In the spring, it's a picture with trees all in bloom
with its rolling grassy slopes.
The children have lots and lots of room
summer sports, PE and games underneath the trees
autumn walks, winter snow brings toboggans all to please
at Christmas time, with sheer delight.
The children take their part with words and music.
Teacher's strive, perfection to achieve.
Parents and friends with pride, will watch.
The scene is set, the magic starts.
The little ones, capture every heart.
It's a beautiful little school, every child's dream.
For there, they quickly learn, with teacher's kind and firm.
For when at eleven it's time to go, on every face, tears do flow.
A better school is hard to find.
Why? Oh why? Must they close it down
and send the children all to town?
In time to come, when the children are grown
and some have little ones of their own.
They'll look back with pride and joy
shed a tear, and wish that little school still here.
So let's bid *farewell*
to dear *Fairley*
and close a chapter in history . . .

Irene G Corbett

REFLECTIONS

To look back on these last five and twenty years;
Is to see again the faces of those who meant so much;
Is to note the shared growth of knowledge that swept away the fears;
Is to reflect on the common purpose and on the lives we touched;
Is to marvel at the kindness of these I could call friend.
Is to remember how few were those I'd never miss;
Is to recall the countless hours that I used to spend
Teaching and guiding students.
How could it end like this?
I need to pay a tribute to all who've worked with me.
Academics, managers and many other staff.
To thank them for their understanding and their generosity.
They gave so very freely that which would be generous by half.
I must also thank those students who came to hear my truth.
Who came to learn of calculus of CPA and such
Who laughed at my jokes and shared with me their youth.
I know I'll miss the College, I'll miss them all so much . . .

M J Scutter

THE ENVIRONMENTALIST!

I am the environmentalist
It's what I have to be.
I'll fight to save the rivers
I'll fight to save the seas
I'll fight to save the meadows
I'll fight to save the trees
I'll fight to save all kinds of life
On land, in sky, in sea.
I am the environmentalist
It's what I have to be . . .

Alan Green

DEATH WITHIN WAR

Death is
a curse upon us all.
It's something we all fear
It's coming for me . . .
Help me please!
. . . Silence!

Amanda Rose (11)

HOMELESS AND HUNGRY

Homeless and hungry
you should have stopped
you know you should
but you just walked on by.
You couldn't face me, face to face
or look me in the eye.
Homeless and hungry
sometimes I think
you wanna help
but you just can't raise a smile.
Got your pockets full of charity
but it's really not your style.
Homeless and hungry
I watch you and
your lame excuses
stumbling through the shame
it's not that you wouldn't if only you could
but it's coming on to rain.
Homeless and hungry
this pathetic sign
around my neck
reduces me to tears.
When everyday I hear you say
these are the golden years.
Homeless and hungry
I've only got
myself to blame
I'm just a waste of space.
A young man living on the street
behind an old man's face.

Rod Trott

GOD IS DIVINE

God knows everything
Yes! He is our king and guide.
We need no other
He is the master of Love.

God knows everything
Yet we ask why do we suffer?
My faith is strong now
Thanks to the Lord.
He has opened my eyes and heart
To the beauty of his Kingdom
God knows everything because
He is the Eternal Father.

Kenneth Mood

YELLOW OCHRE

On the horizon oblivious to the
stars and moon.
The sun magnificent and brilliant
caresses her saffron ball of fire
towards the Earth unaware of
her magnitude framing the
picturesque landscape.
Perhaps the golden chasms will echo
the lemon and oranges drinking the
nectar from magical goblets.
Shielding the delicate plants the yellow
wood graces and covers the shadows
of the beautiful scenery.
In the Earth the yellow pigment waits
to be transported to factory and plant.
The artist comes along to paint or
dye and the world is illuminated
in glorious technicolour.

Then the cowardly creatures
frightened and timid hide
behind the branches of
jasmine and laburnum.
Yellow is the key
positive and dynamic one moment
insipid and watery the next.
Unaware and translucent
the pigment and the wood
shining and golden.
Making bubbles and waterfalls
fill the world
with primroses and sunbeams.

Supposedly forgetful and fleeting.
The goldfinch springs from
bough to bough.
Illuminating the gold fish
in the mirror of the pools below.
Resplendent in their beauty
making the Earth aglow.

Sarah Margaret Munro

THE CHARITY SHOP

Walking down the busy street
in the hot July heat.
To do some shopping was I bent
a bargain-hunting gent.
The urgent traffic's roar
into the sun-filled air did soar.
I passed a shop, or two, or three
and there was nothing there for me.
Then I came upon a Charity Shop
which had a large sign on the top.
The door was standing open wide
inviting anyone to come inside.
For sale was many a thing,
whatever people there could bring.
Some books were very cheap
piled on the floor in a heap.
There were clothes and odds and ends
that one could buy for one's poor friends.
There were tapes that one could play
at home on a gloomy sad day.
Happy was my searching time
when I found a book on rhyme.

W Fred Tabaczynski

Is Your Confidence Misplaced?

Angry men will show surprise
If all hope is lost
For a feeling of trust
Is now a losing desire
A high expectation
Is a healthy outlook
If only your belief
Is attainable.

Warren Brown

SHIPWRECK

Seven long years
We've been here
Living on coconuts
Fish and beer.

Our ship was wrecked
And washed ashore
With barrels of beer
And rum galore.

This island shore
Of sun, sand and sea
In England we would
Rather be.

Adrian Newport

RETIREMENT

If you are retired and living on your own
Your partner has departed and you feel all alone
You get yourself a routine of things to do each day
It will help you to feel useful and keep the blues away.
You'll start to have a restful sleep and wake up feeling good
Then you go jogging in the park, before eating any food.
Then you have a shower and you feel really fresh
You are now ready to face the day, not having any stress
Then you eat the right food, that is cholesterol-free
And drink lots of water instead of cups of tea
Then you do a little exercise, not anything too hard
Just trimming round the garden or brushing up the yard
Some people are happy just to live a life of wealth
But there's nothing more important than keeping in good health.

Keena

A Daughter's Love For Her Father
(For my late father Anwar Hussain)

I knew one day that you'd depart,
and leave me with a grieving heart,
despite the things I'd said to you,
the doctor's confirmed what I knew.

Many asked just how I felt,
my mind and body to tears would melt,
you retreated to your place of birth,
your soul departed from this earth.

For many a night I could not sleep,
the image of you, my thoughts would keep,
nothing did I feel but pain,
tears flowed freely, like pouring rain.

You vowed to me you'd never go,
and since you went I'm cold as snow,
each day I've tried to drown my sorrow,
but each day soon becomes tomorrow.

Behind you left children and wife,
leaving us all to deal with life,
the children whom you most adored,
now feel empty, alone and bored.

Without you what does the future hold?
I doubt if it's a pot of gold!
Each day and night I pray for you,
hoping your spirit will see us through.

December the 14th. I'll never forget,
as now we're filled with deep regret,
to speak of you just makes me sad,
because I still want my loving dad!

Farhana Hussain Begum

FACETS OF A HORSE

A horse, flowing tail, swirling mane,
Flaring nostrils
Running flat out on plain.

Freedom curtailed, lassoed, broken in
By cowboys to herd
Cattle to acres, virgin.

Used by diddicoys, tinkers of the road,
Even a trot
Too fast and slowed.

Pulled light field guns, when countries at war,
Milk and bakers' carts
Halting door to door.

Ridden by children, especially disabled,
Therapeutic to ride
Beside those who are abled.

Side-saddled by Queen at Trooping Colour,
Artists' models
For oil, watercolours.

Racing on flat or over the jumps
Oft' tossed the jockeys
To ground with loud thumps.

Grazing, trotting, neither saddle nor reins,
Dreaming he's first
In the field, his one aim.

Later become stud
A horse's ambition
Then in time, follow
Red Rum, a sire's mission.

Hilary Jill Robson

THE PHOTOGRAPH

Silver and oval is the frame surrounding you, you're captured
in a second, no time could steal the youth in you. What were your
thoughts, your feelings, the dreams you held inside your heart?
Is it that you fulfilled them or did they all just fall apart?
Your eyes, they seem to watch me, I wonder if you'll start to move,
then walk towards that background to then vanish out of view, you're
only in a photo till it crumbles all away, just like your life that's gone
now, no future years can ever replay. After your photo was taken,
what did you do? Where did you go? Did you ever stop to wonder
where you would be when as a soul? and that that very photo might still
be around today, to remind all of your memory and wonder what you
did that day.

Sandra Brisck

HE WAS ON THAT BOAT, THE HOOD

He was on that boat The Hood - my boy who died!
And looking at that note - that should they have supplied . . . ?
'Twenty years old . . . by a fraction!
Missing! . . . Presumed killed in action!
Errors permitting . . .
Nothing left afloat!'
Was he near a boiler down below?
Or by a magazine positioned so?
Halfway up a staircase - back of the lot?
Snuffed out like a moth that's soon forgot!

Deep inside her bowels their faces stare . . .
Knowing they must sweat their torsos bare . . .
The gauges bend, each engine growls -
With everything its got!
Before the walls turn blue -
And then white-hot!
'I love you . . . Mum!'
He said, to ease my pain . . .
'Don't look so glum . . .
I'll soon be home again!'

Tom Ritchie

LONELINESS

Loneliness is what I feel when you're not there,
A feeling of lacking, being incomplete.

Since the first time our eyes met,
I knew we were meant to be,
Together forever and ever more to come.

I can only hope and pray for your return,
When once again I will feel complete.

Ben Morgan

PEOPLE BEING IN DEBT

People being in
Debt
Are never
Set
To have a
Bright future
For the Loan Sharks
Think it is
Right
To ask for
Money
Because that's their
Bread and
Honey
But if the
People in
Debt
Say 'No'
The Loan Sharks
Would not be
Able to open their
Door.

Coleen Bradshaw

JO - SIMON

Oh my little Jo
How I've seen you grow
From a baby to 'Miss know it all' now
Although you're only eleven
I used to teach you to dance
To wiggle your bum, I showed you how it's done.
You kept me awake at night
My fault I think, a 'Jack in the box'
You play at two in the morning
Sleep, I might have got
If I'd left him in the shop.

Simon, my six foot grandson
Painted yourself green to match the grass
Mum could not move as to her you clung
Now you chase the girls for kisses
As you think your old nan's past her prime.

Well my Jo and Simon, you have a long way to go
Jo, thanks for coming to help me in the garden
The jobs you do Simon, thank you too
Because you're both the best
Even though you think I'm past my time.

Evelyn Farr

FUTILITY

Why
Are
Rivals

Shooting
Attacking
Destroying

Wanting
A
Rammy

Bombing
Ambushing
Decimating

What
A
Rabble

Macho
And
Disastrous

Make-up
And
Disband

Match
And
Disperse.

Stan Short

THE DAY I WAS SO SCARED

I was cruising in a big ship and there was a man, that every morning he jumped in the sea for a long swim. But one day he jumped but he never returned at the usual time. I looked for him but I could not find him. Suddenly I saw him fighting with a big wave, I told myself that he was in danger. I started to scream for help. A few people came and asked me what had happened. I told them 'Look at that man, he is fighting to come out.' They looked and they were all laughing at me. I said ' Why are you laughing, the man is in danger.' They said 'Do you know his name?' I said 'No.' They said 'He is the only man to survive the deep dive in any big sea or ocean. He is the best expert of the sea.' And they were still laughing at me. I said 'I did not know all that, I was worried and concerned for the man.' They afterwards told the gentleman and he thanked me and had a good laugh too. But for me it was a shocking time at that moment of my life. They offered me a drink and we became good friends.

Antonio Martorelli

PROTESTER

Don't call me Crusty
Don't call me Smelly
I am just a human
I might look a bit odd
But I am a protester
To save our planet
Against all evil
Who ravish our planet
It does not matter
I do not really care
What I look like!
I just save our planet
I wear funny clothes
But I am just a human being.

Bob Lewis

Spring Scene

The eagerly awaited spring scene
Bare shoots are studded
With fresh leaves of pea-green
Lighter days, with colour to see
And nesting birds at dawn
Conduct a symphony.

The evergreen shrub choisya terrata gives
Citrus scent from starry white blooms
Whilst clematis apple blossom
Dons a cloak of almond perfume
Primroses and forget-me-nots, beautiful
Shade of blue.

Delightful lily-of-the-valley
Multitudes of creamy white bells
Orange aniseed - fragrant wallflowers adorned
With scented, golden jonquil daffodils
Yellow and white chaliced tulip tarda
Is really unforgettable.

To the crooning of a woodland dove
Lovers stroll hand in hand together
Sweet innocence of young love
Hopeful their dreams will last forever
Pause, by the hillside to survey
Lambs frisk and play.

Joan Taylor

LITTLE ANGELS

An angel, a cherub, a sleeping child or maybe two.
Can be found in the old master's paintings and sculpture too
But in real life you can still see them embodied here
For they exist in all little children far and near.
If you are fortunate enough to have children yourself
You'd have seen often your child asleep, innocence itself.
Who has not crept into the room at night, to take a peep.
And stopped to admire them laying in sleep so deep.
So peaceful, quiet, clean and beautiful, such a setting.
A reminder of angels and cherubs, of the paintings.

Terry Daley

Pongamegunk

The Pongamegunk is a terrible creature,
Horrid and cunning and mean,
That slithery, slimy, crafty beast
Who's so clever, he'll never be seen.

He hides in my lunch box, he hides in my boots,
And often he's under my bed
Amidst crisp packets, sweaty socks,
Gloopy and Loopy,
My goldfish who long have been dead.

Why I get the blame
When Pongamegunk is the culprit
I really can't see.
'Go and wash!' shouts my mum,
'You smell just like a skunk.'
'That's the Pongamegunk, it's not me!'

I search in my backpack,
There's nothing much in there
Apart from an old apple core.
But the nasty niff that wafts out of my bag
Tells me Pongamegunk's in there once more.

Get out of my pocket, old Pongamegunk,
You leave my egg sandwich be.
I know it's quite old
And is now growing mould,
But it's my midnight snack, don't you see?

Why must he creep into my wastepaper bin,
Making it sticky and smelly?
He's after the sausage that I threw in there,
And that raspberry flavoured jelly.

You smellygunk, stinkygunk, Pongamegunk,
Go and find somewhere else to stay,
For I'm tired of you and the things that you do,
Making trouble for me every day.

Does anyone here have a Pongamegunk,
Who pesters you time after time?
If you haven't, I've got one,
I really don't want him,
So you are quite welcome to mine!

Janet Randall

SUBMISSIONS INVITED
SOMETHING FOR EVERYONE

ANCHOR BOOKS '99 - Any subject, light-hearted clean fun, nothing unprintable please.

WOMENSWORDS '99 - Strictly women, have your say the female way!

STRONGWORDS '99 - Warning! Age restriction, must be between 16-24, opinionated and have strong views. (Not for the faint-hearted)

All poems no longer than 30 lines.
Always welcome! No fee!
Cash Prizes to be won!

Mark your envelope (eg *Poetry Now)* **'99**
Send to:
Forward Press Ltd
Remus House, Coltsfoot Drive
Woodston
Peterborough, PE2 9JX

OVER £10,000 POETRY PRIZES TO BE WON!
Judging will take place in October 1999